UNCEDED LAND

UNCEDED LAND

Issam Zineh (signature)

poems by Issam Zineh

THP

For Anthony – With thanks for
your support. Congratulations on
" Burnt Spoon Burnt Honey!" Wishing
for great things for your poems.

–IZ
Baltimore '22

Zineh, Issam
1st edition

ISBN: 978-1-949487-12-1
Library of Congress Control Number: 2021951011

Interior design by Matt Mauch, Natasha Kane and Sarah Dumitrascu
Cover art by Julia Soboleva
Cover design by Joel Coggins
Editing by Tayve Neese and Natasha Kane

Trio House Press, Inc.
Ponte Vedra Beach, FL

To contact the author, send an email to tayveneese@gmail.com or visit www.issamzineh.com

For Joseph DeRoche, lovingly

TABLE OF CONTENTS

I.

I am the land in a body
you shall not pass

– Mahmoud Darwish

Rare Bird

Three boys from the refugee camp
next to my uncle's house are whipping

a pigeon. They are dusty. I can see
they're wearing the same clothes

from the day before. The bird is dusty.
It's not going anywhere. A broken

bird trying to get off the ground sounds like
a rolled-up paper through air, like errant skin.

You ask me to be more intentional.
Today: work *cicatrix* into conversation.

Show me your scar, now your limbs—
show me what it is that obsesses.

Ask one question that won't be answered:
What is it about these parts?

Enumerate the invisible: not private struggle,
which has its own airglow. Not exactly

the smoke from the fire that zippered more
than it crackled. Not the escape tunnel that led out

from the concentration camp. Not the memory of *sea*
when we came across seaweed washed up on shore.

These all have their signs and symbols—some way
to point to, at least, the semblance of the thing in question.

The truly unseen—how when I say no one had ever
touched me before, you think of the pyracantha we never planted.

The grass is a little taller and the clothesline
a little slacker. How there is a certain

strength in naming that owes wholly to the intention.
How the wind whispers *liberate.*

Catastrophic Sonnet

[My grandfather still has his house key from 1948. He says he lives in the part of the village where the past doesn't kill you. He invites his neighbors in for fruit and mixed nuts and something cool then something hot. There is a belligerence of songbirds every square mile. *Come see what I brought you from the market,* he says: cucumbers, local, pomegranates, za'atar. *I see you've renounced your birthplace, which is of course your right. When they come for you, they will ask about your love's name, her contours, her address. You will dream of male sunbirds feeding on nectar mid-air.* Where is it written that we're supposed to call? I misheard him talk of our rightful place at the top of the hill. My kids fell in love with imperialism last summer in London. They discovered legacy in the gardens. They woke to the logics of the enterprise. I miss the burgers at Johnny's]   .

Unceded Land

This part of the cape is known for oysters. That part's known for turnips.
The playhouse is closed until next season. I keep reporting in this way.

    fort   hill   rock   harbor

We stand at the edge of town cove. You ask why
I brought you here and if I remember any of the original intensity.

The sun is a kind of gratitude, you say, a continuously
   ringing bell in the lower belly that we can breathe right into.

You have done it again, this time without the modesty
it might require: taken your cresting pain and turned it into a kite.

You will come clean if I ask.

We should start seeing goldfinches this time of year.
How would you describe a warble to someone who has never heard one?

A music without words, a euphemism in the cessation of sound,
a scarce Bedouin music where we are in tents and pour each other out,

bloated, amorous, into little bone cups for drinking.

                                        I say,
      we might be standing on unceded land.

Light in a field.
              You say, *I have no need*
                  of such things. Just sing to me, baby, just sing.

There are New Names for God

Your mother invents a celestial archetype for your benefit.

She soaps her thighs in the bathtub—
thinks about which subway worker flips the switch
that shifts the track. Some man with man
hands that could asphyxiate her in an eroticism
she's only imagined as an appalling list.

Adagio

Beginning is like tracing lamplit ellipses. The wall against your finger

tells of fresh heat settled over a room we do not own and don't care to.

The processional sweat of night makes this bed the bottom of a body of water.

Behind your head, the seawall—static, insomniac—maintains against what erodes.

Crumbling quiet is the measure of your voice, your immortal torso,

the mercy of your legs around me. We've made something of our selves.

Extending at the elbows until all that is left is extension. Euphony

bends without angle: this nameless part of your throat. We have left behind theme:

air, a dance of vengeance, a quiet city, an old man's collected songs where every verse

is grief in the tempest of a stolen bucket. And you can arrange to forget my face.

Lips might be nothing more than shadow waiting for day, bodiless as song.

The human mouth fills with foam. I will make something of you.

For your body, a slow stretch of bow across beauty bedded down in sound.

Your body, like a long vowel held in the composition of my breath.

Asking for a Friend

She would be flying into town later that day to stay with us. There was no A/C and records were broken that year. Our parents slept on the floor in the living room. We knew she was from some agricultural republic, originally, but that was the extent of it. We would never get around to talking about culture or colonization much. There was one night where she made a point about the power of language to subjugate, something about *mosquito* and *Miskito*. One night, we took turns talking into a fan. I met her brother years later. He was a Red Sox fan. He had a hard time with the "g" in Roger "The Rocket" Clemens. Did he know she was the first woman to put me in her mouth? In her language, "Oh God" sounded a lot like "Goodbye." That summer, we ate corn straight from the can.

My Father Used to Hunt Pheasants & Quail

when I was a kid. I never got to go with him.

You're wearing a new t-shirt.
Two of our three children are sunburned.

Is this what you meant by revelation?

Citrine

What little I knew about commodity
I learned from my father. We traded in broken bones.

Felt every mineral surface. Felt the dark. Not darkness.
There's that difference between dark and darkness—

a mouthful of earth, the same primordial egg within us
out of which all forms arise, then return to in time.

When I was 8 or 9, my prized possession was a 4 x 6
piece of cardboard with rocks and gemstones glued to it.

I'd carry it in my backpack every day, memorize
the scientific and popular names of each specimen.

I loved how everything had 2 names.
Now you can buy your kids collections

of pre-historic shark teeth and meteorite fragments.
They come with detailed learning guides.

I never thanked you for the citrine you sent
to the house. The handwritten note was lovely.

I didn't understand what you meant at the time
but now it's different. When you wrote *just a little something*,

I think you meant: *When I cry, I don't cry for the inevitable loss.*
When you wrote *good luck*, I think you meant: *I hope you open*

your eyes and find yourself under a tree laden with fruit
you cannot name. I imagine you outliving me.

My daughter is now the age I was then.
She passes that citrine all gold and white

through her hands. When she asks where I got it—
sometimes I say I found it. Sometimes, I say I bought it a long time ago.

Parable to Keep You Safe, Defy Aging, & Banish Evil:
Every Dream is More Vivid

a Manhattan businessman writes a poem about how pneumonia
killed his wife—calls it *Captain of the Men of Death*

a chorus of redheaded nudes

a brood of chicks with lips for beaks
and the Harlem Boys Choir boys chant *pervert, pervert, Prévert*

Pygmalion ass-fucks himself with a stone he's fashioned for private use

Peacock, Egg Harbor City, New Jersey

The couple that owns this place says the peacock has more than one mate.
And did I know there are plants that bear flowers with stamens only,

some only pistils? Though I see you in the early morning, I imagine you
the same at dusk. Sun and shade, petal and seed head, becoming anything

you can fit into your beak. You are, yourself, an exercise in noticing—
there is the stealth, what was once called *furtive*. The eye-

spotted train that refuses, at least today, to be seen as anything other
than a net of jewels. You've roamed all morning. Your spurs say *try me*.

The rest of you says try again. You are blue as blue has never been—
river water rendered in glass the moment before birth—green

as green has always been—one part territory, one part terror.
You are not only what you are but what you interrupt:

in an RV park. In an American refuge. You are as much *other*
as the movement that made this place. I have seen you before:

served in full plumage in some Flemish painter's allegory;
in Tulum, the day my second daughter was born;

among the Yazidi girls who jumped to their death
from the sacred mountain; as a gorgeous declaration of war.

Ars Poetica

I am married on a cliff. Today, we are
all we want. The future rests on buzz

words, easily broken like an ankle in the sand.
The beauty of it in the mind is an insistence

of sanity on the lanai, a home, a portico, a past.
The day is black and formal. The imagery is

a different matter. The air is salted, the sky like
blueberry yogurt. Later, you would tell me

yogurt turns your stomach—that you liked
skylines and nightlife and violence.

The guests have arrived. We walk down one
path at once, hating, for now, everything that blooms,

knowing this is a small part of the introduction,
an even smaller part of conclusion.

Black Breakfast

In certain restaurants, you can order *black breakfast*.
The waitress will bring coffee and a cigarette.

Our language in this world: pleonasms as
"I saw it with my own eyes." Well, of course
you did. What else? In this way, a little excessive.

You didn't sleep in. You're not hungry.
Not so much *appetite*, you try to explain, as
much as transgression between what is and is

not *mouth* the human craves—that which is
distinguishable from inner dark, but only insofar
as drought is distinguishable from the drought-

stricken. That hunger. There is blood and ash
on the table. Your legs are crossed under, thigh
over thigh. You're thinking about someone

else. He—vast as a colony, and tender still.
We in all the shifting alarms of dawn. Our bodies
are now given their places next to the old

themes: love, loss, the stiff jaws of the dead
and the distressed. We come to accept
natural slip ups, pleasure as a lovely put on,

and, of course, beauty as the slow question
mark in the universe's argument with itself. This sort
of consent, we never come to know, is commendable.

In later years, I remember the good:

The freckles on your forearms.
The feral realism of your bird calls.
The way you take your coffee.

Sappho in California

We can only imagine the rubies
and pearls that were Los Angeles at night.
The plane touches down like a toe testing
the pool water where the city starts.
This is where it might start. We can be sure
as the swallows of San Juan Capistrano.
She doesn't know about the swell of sea salt
that we've mistaken for loops of gulls
around the bay. Everything grows
wild. Everything like a cherry.
Poets come here. No one asks them to come.
Some hate Ashbery, some love him. And she
buries hate like two thoughts, the passive hands
of the Pacific: one version of herself
beneath the floorboards of her father's house.
Leda hiding a swan's egg in a pillow.
In any case, we shouldn't expect much
from this place. This coast will never say
"You have moved me." Children will be born.
Oranges will still grow without us.

Parable to Keep You Safe, Defy Aging, & Banish Evil:
The Inherent Features of the Phenomena of the Physical World

You know nothing of botany. You name the plants.
This one, *carnivore*. This, *pronoun*.
That, *foliage spasm, but barely.*

A tree that bears fruit
in winter. Another with no top.
Someone has been here before and scratched into the bark.

I am there before you.
I do it with your car key.

Metaphor is the Momentum Between Gestures

& I am Coptic,

you are Christ, my heart a slit lamb, punctured,
slick at the throat. The alchemist's optic

obsession: stuff to gold & never back.
Even the vein, sexual, royal purple,

royal, textual: as lunar black
sometimes, on paper, becomes inevitably

smoke white. All the swollen signs of night:
from the full satellite, the early year moons—*wolf, snow*—

to the slow diastole of chest, the right-
hand turn before your house, &, of course, you.

What to do about you? Perhaps a Taj,
wrench an adagio from my rib,

or maybe it's enough to adjust
the pillow under your head. I can give

you my word: in some future I will shake
your husband's hand, hold your face

& say, "It's wonderful to see you
again." We will both turn away in shock,

proud we pulled it off, proud of our disgrace.
We will smile. There will be nothing left

to do except go home
& make love in separate beds.

There will be nothing left but to accept
a world without regard for what is said.

It is the momentum between gestures—& I am
Emmanuel & you are the sepulcher.

In

the
next
lifetime
God

sends down
pills
for his
people

wafers of
biochemistry
to keep us
equal

whip-its
for the
kids
and

for us
for the obsessed

God
rages
with the
orderlies

kingdom
phylum
class
order

and
so on
in-
finity

the ordered
legions
of wings
the

severe
angels push
their hard
bodies

into ours
we begin
to love
them for

their
brutality
for them
knowing

nine ways
to enter
the human
body

this is
for the
girl
they say

who bears
African violets
into the
New World

this
is for
your world
of poetry

Capricorn

Christ did not want to leave the body.
        – Linda Gregg

It must have been hard for him to recount
the parable with her there—just shaved,

mons slick with suds, sweat winging
to her armpits, the serenity of a man

between trees—trees, an ability to forget.
Apple yields fig. Fig yields cypress.

It became a kind of therapy session.
She was in bed. Netting

kept the mosquitoes from her
thighs. As she slept, discovery made

its way in like another snake from the landscape.
She woke to a mercy that came in the form of a fish.

And they ate and were made aware of the beauty
of the animals. This, at least, is how I learned it.

Isn't God a centuries-old sign of wanting,
the swollen remnant of rest?

Isn't guilt the smallness of our bodies
against open space?

Aren't you the welcome blackness
that swallows me whole?

Psalm

turn the lights down low / for the lord has multiplied my love / i have waited in secret and silence, in dark places / in the city's thighs, and he has not shown / this is the point of quiet exclamation / he is not addiction / he is not brutality / not the semi-automatic, not the *tak tak tak tak* of joy or resistance / not Elysium, not elision / he is not the limelight /not the announcing volcano / he is not a sword or funnel / he is not the glad loin or gladiolus / he is not the gold lion in the den / i have waited for him with head cocked / dribbled into his cup and pyx / he is not the place to begin / you are / your body whispers between mine and the most high's / i forget the unholy god whose name is excellent / by you i have known the beauty of the blaspheme / you give meaning, my conceit /

you are all   deliverance   tip   speech

II.

merge our bodies merge
give
wealth / freedom
congress cannot legislate away

– Wanda Coleman

What If a Love Like This

I caught a starfish, second summer after my divorce.
You know it's your fault you
were once again standing off in the dark
on the borderline between sea & soul.

I licked the salt from your neck:
sing me rivers the anthem of blue waters, the hymn
of my eye the coastline disappears on—
then. This is the dark he lives in.

I see myself thrown heart first into this ruin.
I throw the symbols. I make reverberations.
This compulsion to write one's name,
substitute *writer* for *mirror*, *visionary* for *window*, *hack* for *glass*.

No one answers, and that fact is a giant fly buzzing.
Once I tried to hang myself and got terribly ashamed.

Once I tried to hang myself and got terribly ashamed.
I laughed, took off the rag I was wearing.
The doctor asks me what I am. I say, a *non sequitur*. He is suddenly
cool air. Caress the light / my body calls.

I have frequent fantasies about running
over people I don't like. It is the early dawn:
I'm 99% body. My brain has dissolved
into basil and blackthorn.

I become a name caller,
a door thru which I escape / another world.
Smell of fresh wet black earth. A fire. We couldn't breathe.
Until he threw water on me.

Ol' sun he steady whispers.
Provide, he said. Provide.

Provide, he said. Provide
a fresh spray of mist and neon.
Camera action: blood & shoes (remember the mountains of shoes?).
Use people, love things.

I offer you whatever incites my blood, whatever
cratered psyche toast-colored skin and lunar eclipses.
This is the purple dawn,
disharmony in all my parts.

My bowels are in my throat
(can't tell mama about this)
pushed to the floor but max is not max enough.
At the tip of each finger a separate universe.

Living with you, he says, *is like living with a Gauguin.*
Lift me thru my skin.

Lift me thru my skin:
small, unsophisticated country—two hours of
the same ol' cold-blooded bloodlessness.
Too little for too much effort I pursue my dramas / those

stars. There is other life out there. I sense it, a smell, a
hello from months later, a black bird with one red feather—
the Chattahoochee the Cheyenne the Chippewa the Cimarron—
washing six-month's worth of dirt & the devil off.

And the subject of your love? We rain in each other /
darkness parts and a nation's heart is released. I am full.
I'm on uptime / have no resting place / cannot rest—
water listening to how I listen knowing there's a limit.

I thirst for the cold white quench.
Without you this city is a pale rude fiction.

Without you this city is a pale rude fiction.
Your sun paints the skyscrapers downtown in late day. The children
expect this letter to go unmailed as have all the others. I—
I am dying in lala in a blizzard of sun where—

god. In my smoke I call you
to take the outer skin in. Rehumanize it.
My father hoists me over his shoulder, holds me
after. I take cuttings of his hair and kiss the air.

My tongue has grown strong and hard
like twin hearts beating in amber.
All that talk about blackberries was talk.
Will you pay to hear my angst of sob and bathe in it?

Do see / refuse the dark.
There are those still throwing themselves into the sea so-to-speak.

There are those still throwing themselves into the sea, so-to-speak.
Somewhere they are unearthing the evidence—
the dark heart / earth casts up its dead
sky, river, mother. Your tongue plunders my mouth,

my love's isolation, my nation and me. Our bickerings—
is that what she holds against me—your eternal
rampant romantic notions of nobly dying in the cause
where crowns of trees inspired by flame extol the night?

I will speak to the night. It will listen.
Forgive this ruined narrative begging the first chaos out of calm. Let my grief be pure.
The phone rings again. Something clicks. It's dangerous.
They have a warrant out for my arrest.

He's out here somewhere dead ahead, enemy and lover. I am armed.
I will not come to the door.

I will not come to the door.
I hear voices sing and shout, hear bodies.
Bed calls. I sit in the dark in the living room.
I decide I may as well walk to keep warm and am suddenly

buying money orders at the post office.
I believed great and prolonged sex cured cancer. I believed
violence. It is imperative that visionaries see
groves of perfect oranges and streets of stars.

I catch a starfish, second summer after my divorce.
The lotus moon is a lover's wound,
and the crows go by…she's on top.
My sky is painted to look like a ceiling.

It happened so gradual I didn't notice.
We lived off love. It was all we had to eat.

III.

And in another second, had our
contact lasted, I was certain that
there would erupt into speech,
out of all that light and beauty,
some brutal variation of *Look,
baby, I know you.*

– James Baldwin

I Name Your Body (This is Not a Poem About an Olive Tree)

hour of my exoneration
rebounding myth
sequence of senses that antler, tusk, & bone
blood & milk
almanac of unnamed moons
remnant sound of the sentient ocean
vital surrounding billow
reconciled city
near-threatened birds of the plain
headwater to mouth
the Nauset light
the darkest verb
the word for land
what I swallow when you say *swallow*

Backstory

Echo's Prologue

The appearance of the body is never
the way we remember it. The phone voice

is not the unpolished voice of the face.
No one did the pointing out, said *fragrance*,

or helped us understand weights and measures,
or showed us austerity in the rugged countryside.

At least two of our kind are losing themselves
in the woods: one broken by the sound

of her own cause, a missed call every hour
on the hour, the other gradually gone,

a song across a blazing meadow:

Every goodbye is a betrayal.
Every betrayal a flower.

§

Narcissus to Echo

There are universals that hold even after
translation. For example: *one half*

of an ass in each hand. A man
comes into full being before you, a single

god drawn out in silence. Would you pull him
in? Would you have something to trade

for escape, should the need present itself?
What would make the difference?

He brings you breakfast tomorrow, regardless,
curls next to you like a comma, unfurls.

Every time you climb into bed, you will
remember him. Even in the quick thrill

of another man's love. We are all myth.
This is beauty. I am who you sleep with.

§

Narcissus Recounts Events from Childhood

I don't remember my mother and father
sleeping in the same bed. There

was no ecstatic blackout, no further
talk of tomorrow. He didn't stroke her

through darkness: instead, what we call
ravage.
            The image of my mother ripples

in a savage brook, almost drowned. At eleven,
he told me I was conceived in a shower.

He wasn't a very good dresser.

§

Narcissus to Echo

Say: *There is no easy way to say this, so I'm just going to say it.*

Say: *coal-black horses.*

      You smell good—like a nervous deer.

Say: *—so there's no misunderstanding later—*

      I can't love you the way I've assumed you want.

      Look at my body (*remember it*).
      Every muscle should contain you.

Say: *—I'm not sure about kids—*

      Do you know what erasure is?

Say: *saga.*
            Say: *god.*

Say: *servant.*

           Say: *sun.*

eternity.

           journey.

Say: *sickness.*

           Say: *About desire, I will always have the last word.*

Say: *bliss.*

Liriope Gives Narcissus The Talk

On the Madison River, winter
        is a hideous act. The trumpeter swans

furl and un-, extend like periscopes,
        and take to water as nature's perennial myth.

The sun comes up like an artist into
        his wife; a palette knife that spreads

the willful legs of sky, commits to a crisis
        of color. This river can be found on improvised

land. You live in a country of God,
        guns, and country—

where some boys carry
        their own severed hands in their pockets.

Imagine in one hand I hold a red jasper.
        In the other, a snowflake obsidian. I offer them

to you like strange, meticulous fruit. In this story,
        you are the sun. You are the symbol that must reciprocate.

Lexicon

In Arabic, all love songs sung

by men are sung to men. And hung
too many times from the rafters,

the word for towel: بشكير—never
quite short enough for the disarray

of the body's mistakes. To say
dreaming in American Sign Language,

put your index to your temple
and curl, not so hard to manage

the repeated tendons of the hand.
The mandarin poet with official words

of love, skin lit like black woods,
official, absolute space renounced

in the heart, makes space with *poem*
in mind. Let's play this new game.

Hysteria, hysterectomy. Not his, not
his but *hers.* And having said this

I take you as you are. Forever and far
in this difficult language of the world.

Swipe Left to View the Same Image in Visible Light

after Jenny Molberg

there is a fine line between looking and not looking
even finer still the thing said and left unsaid
there's an expression in Arabic that translates to *either shoot him*
or break his brain the closest equivalent to *a bull in a china shop*
with room for interpretation as there might be between, say, *presence* and *embodiment*
the original expression used to go *god* is in the details
avoidance can look something like intention from the outside
my therapist says liberation comes from writing down the details
in one context what is expected in another means a public death
how willing we must have been to take that chance
take for instance what will become of that bowl of fruit you leave out overnight
take for instance what came before you that you forgot you inherited
take for instance what came of an imagined wolf whistle
take for instance what became of that girl who lost a tooth in her dad's knuckle
take for instance what might come from a mistimed recollection
take for one final instance what might come from a split second of noticing
the gaze in its violent shimmering—a knife in the grass—

Parable to Keep You Safe, Defy Aging, & Banish Evil:
Bathroom Graffiti Can Mend a Broken Heart

Jimmy from New Bedford is a cocksucker

Mud thrown to the ground is lost

While you're reading this, your wife
is riding a guy that looks like Che Guevara

Milk the cow that's closest to you

Dress sexy at my funeral

Plastic Bag

I will tonight, god willing, sleep like a
baby. I will dream, the recurring one in
which you wrap me in your arms
and drag me to the bottom of the
lake, hold me underwater until I
either drown or wake. In the
morning, news of a child in a plastic
bag floats across a bloated river,
even now as I see it, without allegory,
unaccompanied, minor.

Parable to Keep You Safe, Defy Aging, & Banish Evil:
Koi Death

A child sees their first koi.

They read later that an average goldfish gets as big as you let it.
Placed in a tank, it grows to a size compatible with tank life.
In a pond, swims to a varied light like an orange banana.

They would afterward hear, over and over, about
big fish in small ponds, small fish in big ponds,
big fish in small fish. A certain recyclable truth.

They will become an astronomer and work late.
They know the sky in Oregon is prettier than it is here.
They understand the cost of achievement—the thing that saves them.

A kid points to their favorite koi in a restaurant known for its
    unusual dinners.

Still Life with Oranges & Goblet of Wine

Even for those who've never heard of *trompe
l'oeil*, there's a sense of being cheated. Think

of Wallace Stevens's sun—a sectioned,
truncated piece of citrus. The rest of us are

stunned by what happened to the forsythia
out back. The asters won't come until summer.

Much has to happen between now and then.
You are a curious uncharacteristic absence.

Here, a couple of unpeeled oranges clenched shut
and somehow receptive to the human version

of hunger. The phallic cackle of the goblet's open
mouth. It's filled with orange Gatorade for effect.

Hitchcock used chocolate syrup for the shower scene
in *Psycho*; felt it more realistic than stage blood.

The open fruit on the table is bright and industrial.
Maybe, in the end, you are not missing.

Zion

The early morning parking lot of the A.M.E.
church is holy—something of grace made flesh
in the black birds that are grace's murder.

This is small town Carolina, the pan-
theist's small-town eye, the nudist coming
to terms with what's missing.

The first crows are a winged down stratosphere,
halve the sky with wings, what was once skyward.
The reason avoidance is worth the having.

    Sparrows at night.

And not just the body. You, having pressed
yourself against me, know its price: doubloons
of pain, prostrate medallions in the in-

finite hulls of the heart,
the galleons that sink to the bottom,
the place where you happen.

Parable to Keep You Safe, Defy Aging, & Banish Evil:
Avoiding Literary Study as a Substitute

You'll come across the following:

> *Poem with One Image*
>
> (an occasional poem to be read before the consummation of marriage)

what you have envisioned	control
to be	shutting off
not pleasure	itself but
the motives for pleasure	common decency
in a room alone what	is pure
uncut adversity	as the front
of my body	smacks against the back

of your body

You'll be asked to comment on *determinacy/indeterminacy*, *rhetoric*, *gender*, and *desire*.

Saturday in Four Parts, with Distance & Equivocation

a streetlamp on at dawn—
an animal skull—
a plastic bag

§

I'm alone, she says, with the kind
of abandon—is it that?—of a child

seeing a 17th-century collection
of art and rarity for the first time,

without her father here to say,
"Come closer. Look, notice the over-

lapping lacquered leather of this Japanese
armor," or her mother in the chamber

of wonders imploring, "Of the purple-
spotted swallowtail, the pink-checked

cattleheart, the Grecian sulphur,
which is your favorite?"

§

We could call it obsession.
How you remind me

about the coming of this full
moon or that. I haven't forgotten.

I know raw light—
know *crow* is an alias.

We could call it terror.
We could call it obligation.

§

There's an unaccustomed
we that sees what lies behind

the *here* and the *now* of the heron's
calculated strike. I crane my neck

toward the slightest unfamiliar sound.
This is how we have come to know

boundary as simply a form of statute.
The question comes from just beyond

an edge of field on fire. All or none.

And then none.

Trigger Warning

When I talk to people on the phone these days and they ask—"How are you?"—I ask if they want the short answer or the long answer. So far, no one has chosen the short answer. Then I tell them about this meme I saw that reads, "Is my house clean? No. But are we having the time of our lives making memories? Also no."

There's a guy that Poetry Twitter is demolishing. Apparently, he's a professor. I think he might even be a Dean. Poetry Twitter says he's a racist. He's reported to have said, "Claudia Rankine has never written a poem in her life." He also allegedly said, "You can't write a poem about a tree these days unless it falls on a person of color."

The term *Middle Eastern* is racist. I did not know that. I'm Middle Eastern. The correct term is *SWANA*. I also learned that from Twitter. Did you know that *Middle Eastern* has "colonial, Eurocentric, and Orientalist origins" and was created "to conflate, contain and dehumanize our people."? I did not know that.

An editor recently polled Twitter about whether they should include a trigger warning in their next issue because of all the pandemic poems.

I've written a poem called "Europa & the Bull." I'm afraid to show it to anyone.

Mass

The combined effects of low mass and dark energy could mean that the universe will expand forever because there is too little mass to provide sufficient gravity to rein it in.
　　– Simon Mitton, *The Lancet*

how if my parents had made different / decisions three decades ago, / it could have been my arm / sticking out of a mass grave
　　– Lenelle Moïse, "Quaking Conversation"

Much has been written about mass—physical property; resistance. In one account, the universe is weighed & found wanting. In another, homes are demolished.

§

When I think *mass*, I think *exemption*. I think *imbalance of lonely body*. I think *old conspiracy*. I think *bluest flame*. I think of how you exchanged your song for someone else's, for the velocity of your own flourishing galaxy. I think *my own irrefutable theory*.

§

Our first nor'easter after moving, my mother & I are caught without shovels. We plow the driveway with an old wooden headboard the previous owners left behind. Hours in she tells me she can see my future. I'll get gout like my grandmother. It will feel like someone separated my big toe from the ball of my foot, placed shards of glass in the joint, reconnected the toe & hit it with a hammer. I'll also have a herniated disc. The pain will be so bad I won't be able to get my dick up. She says you don't have to be a Buddhist to know life is suffering.

§

For the warm, ascended Christ

For my salt-whipped mother who is too much mother & too much wife, whose grief is a suitcase with a body in it

For the five U.S. Army soldiers of the 502nd Infantry who gang raped & murdered the 14-year-old Iraqi girl who shared my sister's name, & killed her father who, for a living, protected the date orchard, & her mother & her baby sister who loved hide-n-seek & the sweet plant in the yard; for these five instruments of change who in the weeks before gawked & gave mom the thumbs up, "Very good. Very good;" who on the day of, weary from playing cards & hitting golf balls into the sun & drinking whiskey & Red Bull, left the checkpoint for the one-bedroom home, broke arms, shot into chests & faces, lifted a dress over a head, tore underwear, lit a body on fire from stomach down; who went out to celebrate their kill with a meal of chicken wings

For our own needs & intentions that we now recall in our hearts [6 second pause], we pray to the Lord: Lord, hear our prayer

§

Do you ever think about our old apartment? How cold it got our last winter together? That night you told me shame was just a point in time. That sometimes you can love someone so much the only way to show it is through violence. That you wanted to unzip my skin & climb into the body.

Word Comes Back

from the temple in Malta.
One of the village girls has snuck in
like a beggar in a forgotten city.

She lies like a house cat on the high
alter, witnessed only by the outdoor
moon and the naughtiest angels.

They pleasure themselves while the milk
is being heated in the kitchen.
Elsewhere, an engineer decides

on the most efficient way to replace
the Sphinx's current lion head
with that of the pharaoh.

The dimensions will be wrong.
What's left will only hint of premeditation.
All relationships are the same

in the beginning. As we get to know
the infinite technology of the body,
nature pares us back to the essentials.

The early billion-neuron burst
scaled to a relative handful
in pyrotechnical brilliance.

The brain's cells: bushmen
with bouquets in their hands.
The invisible tropics that divide

our lobes and cortexes disappear
in the moments immediately after
our first apologies.

We still miss each other sometimes.
We look for things that are irretrievable
in minor folds of solitude.

We fire, we flood, we famine.
We don't know much
of petal or stamen,

the easiest of metaphors,
the easiest sounds the tongue
can make. And still,

God has set up its system.
Proteins are synthesized and sent
to correct destinations. The awfully

beautiful things of the body
go on happening. The embarrassment
of the thighs' musk is over.

We are mutually exclusive.
There is one less secret to keep.
You rethink your idea of God:

as lexicon, a plastic bag,
a milder form of kindness.

You Ask If I'm Ready to Die for a Metaphor

My cousin burns
half his face right off his skull smoking
cigarettes and huffing fumes on the roof.

I push a baby stroller over the exposed roots
of a red maple forest as you light the escape fire.

I need more examples.

You curl your hair behind your ear,
show me your growing stack of fiction

body after body rising from the cold spring.

Coefficients of Friction

The physicist in me,
with polymers mated against steel thrust

washer geometry, in all my traction, grip, and desire,
is trapped in the wrong version of eternity.

You are valuable and dimensionless.
Load and velocity.

Somehow, we manage the perpendiculars
that push us: classic form, controlled damage,

a growing evidence of others.
While we fuck, you remember the lions

of Tsavo, *a hunger wholly justified*
by the cruelty of the colony—how it happens

that the brittle bones of resistance
offer little by way of deliverance.

The animal's rictus. Lioness with a broken
sheering tooth, apex and insatiate.

You ask if what we know of each other
is literal, say your body is indigenous

and insist I acknowledge the land I'm on.
Then I wake. This is the latest version of the dream.

The basic requirement for movement
is two surfaces: flight is / underwing /

air / a girl on the run / rubber / road
beauty against bone / empire

We believe ourselves nations.
I come to you because I want to come

and because coming is as much
a going away from.

Measurement is its own form of witness.
Tabulate. Immortalize me.

Notes

Page 13. *Catastrophic Sonnet*: The title alludes to the *Nakba* ("catastrophe")—the displacement of hundreds of thousands of Palestinian Arabs from their homes and lands in and around 1948. The poem modifies a line from Waleed Sayf's "Death at Night's End" translated by Elmusa and Heath-Stubbs (see Salma Khadra Jayyusi's *Anthology of Modern Palestinian Literature*, Columbia University Press, 1992).

Page 16. *Adagio*: Lines 8-10 are a composite of titles from musical compositions by Bach, Barber, Copland, and Schnittke.

Page 19. *Citrine* modifies a line from Sinan Antoon's *The Book of Collateral Damage* translated by Jonathan Wright (Yale University Press, 2019).

Page 21. *Peacock, Egg Harbor City, New Jersey*: Egg Harbor City, NJ was originally established by Americans of German descent fleeing religious persecution and anti-immigrant violence from the far right, nativist "Know Nothing" movement. The last stanza alludes to Brueghel the Elder's painting *Allegory of Taste, Hearing and Touch* (ca. 1620), the Yazidi's Melek Taus (Peacock Angel), and the peacock vehicle used by the Hindu God of War (Kartikeya).

Page 29. *Capricorn*: The epigraph comes from Linda Gregg's "Christ Loved Being Housed."

Pages 34–40. *What If a Love Like This*: This sonnet crown is a cento. The poetry of Wanda Coleman serves as the source material.

Pages 45–48. *Backstory* and *Liriope Gives Narcissus* The Talk borrow from and reimagine the myth of Echo & Narcissus as I have come to it through Edith Hamilton's *Mythology* (Warner Books, 1999) and Ovid's *The Metamorphoses: A Complete New Version* translated by Horace Gregory (Penguin Books, 1960).

Page 49. *Lexicon*: The Arabic word for towel (بشكير) is pronounced "bashkeer."

Page 50. *Swipe Left to View the Same Image in Visible Light*: The poem's title comes from a NASA Instagram post in which two Hubble telescope images of the Eagle Nebula's Pillars of Creation are shown side by side (one in infrared and one in visible light). The poem's first and last lines are after Jenny Molberg's "Epistle from the Funambulist Hospital for Invisibility" (from *Refusal*, LSU Press, 2020).

Page 52. *Plastic Bag* hopes to memorialize Óscar Alberto Martínez Ramírez and his 23-month-old daughter, Valeria, who drowned in June 2019 trying to cross the Rio Grande. Their story garnered worldwide attention in large part due to a photo by Julia Le Duc/Associated Press.

Page 54. *Still Life with Oranges & Goblet of Wine*: The title comes from a painting by John Frederick Peto (1854-1907).

Page 59. *Trigger Warning*: The quoted text on the term *Middle Eastern* comes from the SWANA Alliance website (swanaalliance.com).

Pages 60–61. *Mass:* An early draft of this poem took formal inspiration from Sun Yung Shin's "Valley, Uncanny." Simon Mitton's article appeared in 2001. The poem alludes to war crimes perpetrated against Abeer Qassim Hamza al-Janabi and her family in Al-Mahmoudiyah, Iraq in 2006. The line that begins "For our own needs and intentions…" comes from an online repository of petition prayers to be offered up during Catholic Mass (prayerist.com).

The title of the *Parable to Keep You Safe, Defy Aging, & Banish Evil* series was inspired by a tabloid newspaper cover from 2002. The concepts of *determinacy/indeterminacy*, *rhetoric*, *gender*, and *desire* in *Avoiding Literary Study as a Substitute* (page 56) are chapters in Frank Lentricchia's and Thomas McLaughlin's *Critical Terms for Literary Study* (University of Chicago Press, 1995).

The quoted texts from Mahmoud Darwish, Wanda Coleman, and James Baldwin that begin each section are from "Poem of the Land," "About God & Things," and *Giovanni's Room*, respectively.

Acknowledgments

Grateful acknowledgment is made to the editors of the following for first publishing some of these poems, sometimes in earlier forms and under different titles:

BAHR: "Mass"
Bear Review: "Swipe Left to View the Same Image in Visible Light"
Clockhouse: "Sappho in California"
EcoTheo Review: "Psalm"
Ethel: elements of "Liriope Gives Narcissus *The Talk*"
FERAL: "Adagio," "In," "Metaphor is the Momentum Between Gestures"
Fjords Review: "Black Breakfast"
FRiGG Magazine: "Ars Poetica," "Saturday in Four Parts, with Distance & Equivocation," "Still Life with Oranges & Goblet of Wine," "Zion"
Glass: A Journal of Poetry (Poets Resist): "Plastic Bag"
Guesthouse: "Asking for a Friend," "Backstory," elements of "Liriope Gives Narcissus *The Talk*"
Lunch Ticket: "Catastrophic Sonnet," "Peacock, Egg Harbor City, New Jersey"
Poet Lore: "Lexicon"
Psaltery & Lyre: "Parable to Keep You Safe, Defy Aging, & Banish Evil," "There are New Names for God," "Word Comes Back"
Spectrum Magazine: "Coefficients of Friction"
Sporklet: "What If a Love Like This"
Tahoma Literary Review: "Unceded Land"
The Rumpus: "You Ask If I'm Ready to Die for a Metaphor"
Tinderbox Poetry Journal: "Rare Bird"

The Moment of Greatest Alienation, a chapbook containing some of these poems, was published by Ethel Zine & Micropress (2021).

About the Author

Issam Zineh is a Palestinian-American poet and scientist. His poems often engage with territory as both demarcated physical and psychological spaces and explore associated concepts: boundaries, identity, power, subjugation, resistance, and reconciliation. The son of immigrants, he was born in Los Angeles and has lived in New England, the Mid-Atlantic, and Southern U.S. He currently lives on the ancestral homeland of the Paskestikweya people. His poems appear or are forthcoming in *AGNI, Guernica, Gulf Coast, Pleiades, Tahoma Literary Review*, and elsewhere. Find him at issamzineh.com.

Thanks

I wish to honor and acknowledge the stewards of the lands, often unceded, on which I've been privileged to live, and which have shaped these poems over many years. These include, but are not limited to, the Gabrielino/Tongva; the Wampanoag, Massachusett, and Nauset; the Shakori, Eno, and Tuscarora; the Seminole and Timucua; the Paskestikweya; and the Palestinians.

My deep gratitude to the wonderful people at Trio House Press, especially Tayve Neese, Matt Mauch, Sara Lefsyk, Natasha Kane, Sarah Dumitrascu, and Annie Grimes for their vision, enthusiasm, and dedication to this project.

Many of these poems are better off for having come across compassionate and keen intelligences. For that, I thank Kazim Ali, Erica Charis-Molling, Christian Collier, Blas Falconer, Vievee Francis, April Goldman, Paula Harris, Sadia Hassan, Stefanie Kirby, Tyler Mills, Megan Pinto, Elizabeth Robinson, Sara Schlossman, KMA Sullivan, Ginny Threefoot, Shannon K. Winston, Alicia Wright, and Mark Wunderlich. Special thanks to Kazim Ali, Ruth Awad, and Tyler Mills whose kind words accompanied this book into the world.

Thank you to Adele Elise Williams for her deep commitment to this collection. I am also grateful to Eloisa Amezcua and Esteban Rodriguez for their help in shaping its trajectory early on.

Thank you to the *Community of Writers* at Olympic Valley. Heartfelt thanks to Erik "Advocate of Wordz" Maldonado and the Nuyorican Poets Café.

This book owes immeasurably to my family, blood and otherwise. Enduring gratitude to my parents, Abir, Ramzi, Laith, and Manny for their love and support. Much love to Danny Bellinger, Meta DuEwa Jones, Andy Eaton, Dave Kotinsley, Carling McManus, and Anna Lena Phillips Bell. Gratitude and love beyond metaphor to Amber Beitelshees, Daphne Zineh, Miranda Zineh, and Gisele Zineh for a life outside of time and the motivation to do this work.

Thank you to my precious fellow traveler Maryama Humbert Antoine. Thank you to Kate Sweeney for boundless openness and for treating these poems as your own.

About the Book

Unceded Land was designed at Trio House Press through the collaboration of:

Tayve Neese, Lead Editor
Matt Mauch, Managing Designer
Natasha Kane, Supporting Editor and Interior Design
Joel Coggins, Cover Design
Julia Soboleva, Cover Art
Sarah Dumitrascu, Interior Design

The text is set in Adobe Caslon Pro.

The publication of this book is made possible, whole or in part, by the generous support of the following individuals or agencies:

Anonymous

About the Press

Trio House Press is an independent literary press publishing three or more collections of poems annually. Our mission is to promote poetry as a literary art enhancing culture and the human experience. We offer two annual poetry awards: the Trio Award for First of Second Book for emerging poets, and the Louise Bogan Award for Artistic Merit and Excellence for a book of poems contributing in an innovative and distinct way to American poetry. All manuscripts submitted to the annual contests are considered for publication.

Trio House Press adheres to and supports all ethical standards and guidelines outlined by the CLMP.

Trio House Press, Inc. is dedicated to the promotion of poetry as literary art, which enhances the human experience and its culture. We contribute in an innovative and distinct way to poetry by publishing emerging and established poets, providing educational materials, and fostering the artistic process of writing poetry. For further information, or to consider making a donation to Trio House Press, please visit us online at www.triohousepress.org.

Other Trio House Press books you might enjoy:

Bloomer by Jessica Hincapie / 2022 Louise Bogan Award Winner selected by Lee Ann Roripaugh

The Fallow by Megan Neville / 2022 Trio Award Winner selected by Steve Healey

The Traditional Feel of the Ballroom by Hannah Rebecca Gamble / 2021

Third Winter in Our Second Country by Andres Rojas / 2021

Sweet Beast by Gabriella R. Tallmadge / 2020 Louise Bogan Award Winner selected by Sandy Longhorn

Songbox by Kirk Wilson / 2020 Trio Award Winner selected by Malena Mörling

YOU DO NOT HAVE TO BE GOOD by Madeleine Barnes / 2020

X-Rays and Other Landscapes by Kyle McCord / 2019

Threed, This Road Not Damascus by Tamara J. Madison / 2019

My Afmerica by Artress Bethany White / 2018 Trio Award Winner selected by Sun Yung Shin

Waiting for the Wreck to Burn by Michele Battiste / 2018 Louise Bogan Award Winner selected by Jeff Friedman

Cleave by Pamel Johnson Parker / 2018 Trio Award Winner selected by Jennifer Barber

Two Towns Over by Darren C. Demaree / 2018 Louise Bogan Award Winner selected by Campbell McGrath

Bird~Brain by Matt Mauch / 2017

Dark Tussock Moth by Mary Cisper / 2016 Trio Award Winner selected by Bhisham Bherwani

The Short Drive Home by Joe Osterhaus / 2016 Louise Bogan Award Winner selected by Chard DeNiord

Break the Habit by Tara Betts / 2016

Bone Music by Stephen Cramer / 2015 Louise Bogan Award Winner selected by Kimiko Hahn

Rigging a Chevy into a Time Machine and Other Ways to Escape a Plague by Carolyn Hembree / 2015 Trio Award Winner selected by Neil Shepard

Magpies in the Valley of Oleanders by Kyle McCord / 2015

Your Immaculate Heart by Annmarie O'Connell / 2015

The Alchemy of My Mortal Form by Sandy Longhorn / 2014 Louise Bogan Award Winner selected by Peter Campion

What the Night Numbered by Bradford Tice / 2014 Trio Award Winner selected by Carol Frost

Flight of August by Lawrence Eby / 2013 Louise Bogan Award Winner selected by Joan Houlihan

The Consolations by John W. Evans / 2013 Trio Award Winner selected by Mihaela Moscaliuc

Fellow Odd Fellow by Stephen Riel / 2013

Clay by David Groff / 2012 Louise Bogan Award Winner selected by Michael Waters

Gold Passage by Iris Jamahl Dunkle / 2012 Trio Award Winner selected by Ross Gay

If You're Lucky Is a Theory of Mine by Matt Mauch / 2012

CPSIA information can be obtained
at www.ICGtesting.com
Printed in the USA
JSHW031453210522
26053JS00006B/176